THE MONSTER DEN

By John Ciardi

THE MONSTER DEN

OR LOOK WHAT HAPPENED AT MY HOUSE — AND TO IT

JOHN CIARDI

DRAWINGS BY EDWARD GOREY

WORDSONG

Acknowledgment: Some of these poems first appeared in *Saturday Review*

Text copyright © 1963, 1964, 1966 by John Ciardi
Copyright renewed 1991 by Judith H. Ciardi
Illustrations copyright © 1966 by Edward Gorey
All rights reserved
Published by Wordsong
Boyds Mills Press, Inc.
A Highlights Company
910 Church Street
Honesdale, Pennsylvania 18431
Originally published by J.B. Lippincott Company

Publisher Cataloging-in-Publication Data
Ciardi, John, 1916-1986.
    The monster den: or, look what happened at my house—and to it/by John
Ciardi; drawings by Edward Gorey.
        64p. : ill. ; cm.
    First published by J.B. Lippincott Company, Phila.
Summary: A collection of humorous poetry.
ISBN 1-878093-35-5
1. Children's poetry—American. [1. American poetry.] I. Gorey, Edward,
1925- , ill. II. Title.
811/.54—dc20   1991
LC Card Number 90-85904

Printed in China

For Benn, Jonnel, and Myra for whom I wrote the first three poems just as if they were really people-children (after which the truth comes out). But anyhow with (shudder) love from

Daddy
1966

And for Sarah Judith, the new member of the Monster Den, who joined us twenty-five years later.

Juby
1991

TIME LEAVES NO TIME WHEN YOU'RE
A BOY

*J*ust being a boy takes all (about)
*O*f every day and half the night
*H*urrying off, on, by, in, out,
*N*ear, far, around, through, left, and right.

*L*earning never to say *please,*
*Y*essir, thank you, how are you?
*L*eaves little time for climbing trees,
*E*gg throwing, and things you *have* to do.

*P*ut yourself in a boy's shoes—
*R*emember (or shall I remind you?)
*I*t takes time to learn to lose
*T*hings when they're right behind you,
*C*lose a door so that it blows
*H*alf off its hinges, never eat
*E*xcept between meals. Goodness knows,
*T*hat takes time. And, I repeat,
*T*ime leaves no time as a boy grows.

OF HURRICANES, SUMMER DAYS, AND MISS MYRA

*M*ost of what a girl should be
*Y*ou are—most times. When you are,
*R*oses, cloud fluffs, a smooth sea
*A*re open, float, stretch blue and far.

*J*ust a minute ticks by then:
*U*p blows a storm, dark roars the sea,
*D*own comes the sky, the roses shatter.
*I*n less time, then, than it takes me
*T*o say, "Darling, what's the matter?"
*H*urricane's over. You're back again.

WHY I HAVE TO WAIT ALL DAY TO
KISS BENN

*B*eing a boy begins with noise
*E*very morning at six or so.
*N*othing starts as loud as boys.
*N*othing has so far to go.

*A*nd nothing goes faster wherever it's going.
*N*or seems to know less about where that is.
*T*he thing is to go with your whistle blowing
*H*ard as my son Benn blows his.
*O*h, well, I think, it's part of growing:
*N*ight will come. And it does. Like this:
Y-A-W-N!—And that's when I get my kiss.

CONTENTS

THE MONSTER DEN

THE MONSTER DEN

I met your Mummy long ago.
She said, "How do you do?" I said, "Hello!"
And we talked a little about a lot.
And as we talked we sat and thought
A lot or a little. And then, I guess,
I asked her a question, and she said, "Yes."
And what I asked was—let me see—
It must have been "Will you marry me?"
For that's what she did. And I married *her*
With a church and a cake and a ring.
                                    Well, sir,
We left our friends when the cake was gone.
We kept the ring (she has it on)
And we changed our clothes and we took a train
To somewhere, I think. And then a plane
To somewhere else.
                        We thought we were
Living happily ever after, sir,
As the stories say. We didn't know then
We were only starting a MONSTER DEN.
But that's what we did.
                            We had it in mind
To have some children. The human kind
Was what we intended. And I will say
It almost started out that way.

For Monster One was pink as a rose
And looked like a girl, with a button nose,
And giggly eyes, and a crookedy smile.
So we called her Myra—for a while.
And then what happened? She grew and grew
And after a while there was no one but YOU
Where our baby had been.

As for Monster Two,
He looked like a boy, so we called him John.
How could we know what was going on?
He looked like a boy, and a fine one, too.
So we took him home. And he grew and grew.
But he hadn't grown much before we knew
What *looked* like a boy was really YOU!

Mummy cried and hung her head.
"Someone is monstering us!" she said.
"Our house is becoming a Monster Den!"

But we didn't give up. We tried again.
And that time what we got was—Benn!
Yes, YOU!—and were we happy then?

Well, all I shall say is that made three.
And I looked at Mummy and she looked at me.
And we looked again at what we had got.
And we thought a little about a lot
As we took it home. For we knew right then
It isn't really a Monster Den
Until you have at least one Benn!

So there we were with our Monsters Three
Breathing out fire at Mummy and me.

And what did we do? What would *you* do?
Right!
We turned into Monsters, too!

BENN

There once was a Something—a boy, I guess.
At least he didn't wear a dress.
And I guess he was people. He seemed to be.
Not always. But sometimes. Sometimes he
Was more like a bobcat—snarling mad.
And sometimes a small imp—howling bad.
And sometimes a great ape shaking a tree.
And sometimes as sweet as a bird can be
Singing the whole world full of joy.
There are *so* many ways of being a boy.
If he *was* a boy. And he was, I guess.
Most of the people who don't wear a dress
Are boys, I'd say. Well, some are men,
But he was too small—he had just turned ten.
So whatever he was, it had to be
Some sort of boy, you will agree.
He was even a good boy now and then.
And better than that, he was my boy—Benn!

FOR SOMEONE ON HIS
TENTH BIRTHDAY

So you're ten! Why that's *two* numbers old!
(As I hope you know without being told.)
It takes a One and a Zero, too,
To count up someone as old as you.
Just think how many years it has been
Since you started your one-number years. All ten!
(That's a lot to think back to, sir.) And then,
Think how many years it will be
Before you change from two numbers to three!

That's why I have it in mind to say
That TEN is the hugest-of-all birthday,
And maybe the gayest, and maybe the best.
It does change more numbers than all the rest
For at least another ninety years!
(That's something to think about!) So here's
To someone TEN! And here's three cheers
For a boy who has changed from one number to two.
And here's my wish (and may it come true):
May you learn to like soap (here's a sample cake free)
By the time you change from two numbers to three!

MISS PRISS

Whenever Miss Myra walks like this—
(You guess for yourself what way that is)—
John L. and Benn call her Miss Priss
And so does Mummy. And so do I.
(If you guessed how it goes, then you know why.)

THE MYRA SONG

Myra, Myra, sing-song.
  Myra, Myra, gay.
Myra, Myra, skip-along
  Sings all day.

Myra, Myra, gloom-pout.
  Myra, Myra, sad.
Myra, Myra, poke-about,
  Don't feel bad.

Myra, Myra, chatterbox.
  Myra, Myra, busy.
What a clatter Myra talks!
  Makes me dizzy!

Myra, Myra, la-de-da,
  Dressed in Mummy's clothes,
Playing Lady Fa-la-la,
  Looking down her nose.

Myra, Myra, sleepyhead.
  Myra, Myra, tiny.
Myra, Myra, slugabed.
  The nose I kiss is shiny.

Gay-sad-twinkle-star
  Big-Myra-small.
What a *lot* of her there are!
  I love them all.

SPEED ADJUSTMENTS

A man stopped by and he wanted to know
Why my son John had become so slow.

I looked out the window and there was John,
Running so fast he had come and gone
Before I saw him. "Look at him go!"
I said to the man. "Do you call *that* slow?"

"He seems to be fast when he wants to be,"
The man agreed. "It would seem to me
He is one of those two-speed boys. You know—
Sometimes fast and sometimes slow.
He runs a mile in nothing flat.
He can run right out from under his hat
When there's nowhere, really, to go. But yet,
Why does a boy who's fast as a jet
Take all day—and sometimes two—
To get to school? I'm sure that you
Send him to school. But yesterday
He didn't get there. And all he would say
When I asked why, was: he started at eight,
But it took so long he got there late."

"How late?" said I.

                    Said the man, "A day."

"I see," said I, "and I think I may say
He won't be late again. He needs
A little adjustment of his speeds,
And I'm sure I know the place to adjust."

"Well, then, that's that," said he. "I must
Be on my way."   27

"Thank you," said I.
"If you see John as you go by
Would you be so good as to send him in?
There is never a better time to begin
A speed adjustment than right away."

"Agreed, and I will," said the man. "Good day."

And just a few minutes after that
In came John and down he sat:
"You wanted to see me, I understand."

"I did, and I do. But you'll have to stand—
At least at first—for what I need,"
Said I, "for I have to adjust your speed.
And when I'm through adjusting it,
I think you won't much care to sit.
Do you know what I mean?"

                              "Oh, oh," said he.
"I'm afraid I do. Is it going to be
Terribly long before you're through?"

"Why, not at all," said I. "Like you,
I can be speedy sometimes, too."

And soon after that, his speeds were adjusted.
And also the seat of his pants was dusted.
It was busy work, but it didn't take long,
And I double-checked as I went along,
Just to make sure there was nothing wrong.

And whatever *was* wrong, I set it straight.
For since that time he hasn't been late.

WHILE I WAS SHAVING

Daddy, you know that Billy Fitch?
He says his daddy says you're rich.
I know you jingle—your pockets do.
If *you're* rich, then am *I* rich, too?
I don't jingle. Well, some of the time
I have a penny, and maybe a dime,
And I feel in my pocket which is which.
And I can tell. But that's not rich.
And not really a jingle but—sort of—a clink.
Is that the difference, do you think?
You jingle, Daddy. I *like* to hear
The way you jingle loud and clear—
All quarters and fifty cents's, too.
Do you like to feel them like—*as* I do?
(I remembered, didn't I?) And can you
Tell with your fingers which is which?
How loud a jingle is *really* rich?
Are you rich? I *hope* you are.
You bought a thirty-five-cent cigar
Last Sunday morning. If you're rich,
Why is it Mummy hasn't a stitch?
That's what she said today when she bought
A dress and a hat. Did they cost a lot?
How much is this house? Are we going to buy
A new car? Daddy, when you die
May I have the house? (See, I didn't say
"Can": I remembered to say "may.")
Can I, huh? When I'm old as you,
Will I be fat and funny, too?
And will I be rich? That Billy Fitch
Says his father says you're rich.
I *hope* it's true. If it *is* true,
Someday will I be rich as you?

SMALL BENN

Look outside. Do you see Small Benn
Digging a cave to be his den?
He doesn't want to live with us.
He says he's tired of Mummy's fuss.
He says he's tired of Daddy's ways
Of being *reasonable.* He says
Daddy's reasons are much too long,
And they always end with *Benn is wrong.*
He says he may not be too bright
But he'd like some reasons why *Benn is right.*
He says he's tired of Miss Myra Priss.
He says he certainly will not miss
John L.—that he's just a noisy tease.
So he asked for a shovel. He *did* say please.

And he's out there now—has been all day.
And he *has* been digging, I must say.
He says no, he's not going to run away.
He wants his allowance. He wants his food.
But he's going to move into his cave for good.
Except, that is, for snacks, TV,
And maybe when there's company,
Or to get a drink.

—Good luck, Small Benn.
Come in and see us now and then.
At least—I hope—to wash your face.
For a cave is a smudgy sort of place.
And you know the rule—you have to be
Washed and neat to watch TV.
Better yet—for it looks like rain—
Why not come back in again
And rest a while? It's getting late.
You must be tired. The cave can wait.
You *could* sleep here just one more night.
And let me snuggle and tuck you tight.
That's reasonable. And it could be right.
There—right *and* reasonable. No? Well, then,
Whenever you're ready—you say when.
But we want you to know we'll miss you, Benn.

READ THIS BEFORE YOU COME IN

Someone told the Rhino it
Should not come in the house.
"I will just step inside and sit,"
Said the Rhinoceros.

And it smiled a smile as it barged ahead.
Said Someone, "Please walk lightly!"
The Rhino smashed a wall and said,
"Oops! Sorry!"—most politely.

It crashed its head right through a door.
Then, as it shook *that* clear,
Its left hind foot went through the floor.
Down came the chandelier.

"I thought I'd just drop by a while
To see how you were feeling,"
Said the Rhino with a yard-wide smile.
"Oh, dear!—Was that the ceiling?"

"It used to be the ceiling but
The sky looks fine up there.
And really, when the walls are out
We get a lot more air.

"Who wants a floor? What's wrong with grass?
And if a window sticks,
What of it?—Once you've smashed the glass,
That's one less thing to fix.

"But, please, my dear Rhinoceros—
I hate to say this—but,"
Said Someone, "once you're in the house,
Why soon the house is out!"

—Now then, if Someone around here
Wants to stay in *this* house
He had best make it very clear
He's no Rhinoceros.

So far, I am obliged to say,
He leaves some room for doubt.
Please leave us that much room or—*Hey!*
Yes, you, young man—GET OUT!

FIDDLE PRACTICE

I guess you know
Some girls are slow
When it's time for fiddle practice.
Their arms get stiff.
They act as if
They had swallowed a dry cactus.
They don't feel well.
Yes, they can tell
They're about to catch a cold.
Well, that's when I
And Mummy try
To say (and *not to scold*):

Your arms are *not* stiff.
Your throat is *not* sore.
But something, we think, is going to be *if*
We have to tell you this *once more:*
IT'S TIME! So get your fiddle and bow.
And get your excuses done.
And practice that piece you're supposed to know
And haven't even begun!

In an hour or so
She puts her bow
To the strings and saws away.
And it sounds all right
For, say, a cat-fight.
But I couldn't exactly say

That note for note
It's what anyone wrote.
That's when I catch Mummy's eye.
And we shudder a bit
At the sound of it.
And both of us wonder why
We make her do
What she's doing to
The music someone wrote.
And we stuff our ears.
And we say, "Three cheers!"
When we come to the last—well—note:
Let's call it that.
For sharp or flat,
Or squeak, or squawk, or squeeeee,
It's done for today.
And I'm here to say
That's good enough for me.

THE LESSON FOR TONIGHT

which is: *When you do things, do them right.*
        Above all, try to be polite.

When you are at the table
  And you need to kick your brother,
Be as sweet as you are able
  To your Dad and Mother.

Thank them for the lovely food
  In a pleasant voice, and—quick!—
While you're being very good,
  That's the time to kick!

When your brother starts to cry
  Always say—*and do not grin*
As you say it—"My, oh my!
  Did I bump your little shin?"

Dad and Mother, you will find,
  Will say you did just right,
And tell your brother he should mind
  His manners and be more polite.

Now, what's the lesson for tonight?
  Right! *Don't let your badness show!*
Above the table be polite.
  Be yourself below.

Then, when you grow up and find
  People run from you at sight,
You may, for your peace of mind,
  Know you've always been polite.

SLEEPLESS BEAUTY

There once was a girl who never went to bed.
Every next day she had wool in her head.

Soft wool, scratchy wool, white, black, and brown wool.
All colors, all shades, and all of her head full.

Every next night for a week in a row
She never went to bed. She didn't *want* to go.

Every next night for a month, for a year
She never went to bed. I hope it's clear

That every next day the wool in her head
Grew thicker and thicker. And have I said

She never got up and she never lay down?
So she never got to wear her pink nightgown.

And she never had breakfast. (You have to have been
In bed before *that*.) And she never knew when

To stop or to start or to get herself rested.
She just ran around until (maybe you've guessed it)

The wool in her head (all colors, all shades)
Grew, grew, and grew into ninety-nine braids

With nine thousand bobby pins holding them tight.
She was, I must say, a remarkable sight.

Some people might tell you, "Well, now, serves her right!"
But what *I* feel most is: she just wasn't bright.

JOHN THE FIRST

(A Bedtime Story for Monsters)

King John the First
Was terribly cursed.
He had a most unkingly thirst
For muddy water. His appetite
Ran to mutton stew. He loved the sight
Of the greasy stuff. When he gobbled a glob
His eyes would glow and his heart would throb.
"How very vastly delicious it is
To slurp a stew as greasy as this!
Bring me another!" he always said,
"And this time put in a mutton head."

So much for his drink. So much for his food.
His thirst and his taste were almost good
Compared to the way he lived his life.
When he went to the market to buy a wife
(To give one example) did he go
To the Utterly Beautiful Wife Shop? No.
Or the Wise? Or the Good? Or the Just So-So?
He went to the Pigyards and bought a Sow.
She was fifty then. She is ninety now.

She bore him a Puppy instead of a son.
He trained it for hunting. It wouldn't run.
King John the First just said, "What fun!"

She bore him three daughters. One was a Cow.
And one a Kitten. And one a Sow—
Just like her mother. And all had the Mange.

"My horrible darlings, I wouldn't change
A one of you for the best there is,"
Said John the First. "By my Royal Fizz,
By the grease on my beard, and upon my word,
What a wonderfully loathsome pack or herd
This family is. We're as royal as can be.
For everyone here looks a lot like me,
And I am a king. I shall celebrate!
It's at least an hour since last I ate.
Get dinner, Cook! And I'm warning you:
Put plenty of grease in the mutton stew.
And summon the apple of my eye.
When I slurp my stew she likes to be by
To grunt and to squeal and to drool a bit
Till I let her have a taste of it.
And bring me a puddle—not too clean.
You may serve it up in the soup tureen."

—I could tell you more, but let that do.
Some things are a lot like mutton stew:
One sample's enough. You don't want two.

So much I say, for John the First
And his wife and his life and his taste and his thirst.
He had his choice, and he liked the worst.

AND HERE'S WHAT HAPPENED NEXT

or

THOSE THREE

Miss Myra and Small Benn and John L.—those three—
Grew tired of Mummy, grew tired of me,
Grew tired of manners, of baths, and of bed,
And of having to mind us whatever we said
(Which they never did, where they always went late,
Which they never took, which were bad when they ate).

Which is to say, they meant to be rid
Of a lot of things they never did
(Or never on time, or never right)
And so they ran away one night.

They left us a note and in it they said:
"Minding and manners and baths and bed
Have ruined our lives. We are running away.
Good-bye. There is nothing more to say."

And they signed it and left. And so they were rid
Of all those things they never did
(Or never right, or never on time).
Small Benn took a quarter, Miss Myra a dime,
And John L. (who never could save) one cent.
And they bought their tickets and off they went.

They wrote us from Spain, but they sent no news.
They wrote us from Egypt and asked for shoes
(Which we sent them at once, for well we knew
How the hot sand burns when your shoes wear through).

They wrote us from India next to say
How happy they were they had run away.
"We are seeing the world! It is good to be rid
Of all those things we never did—
Minding and manners and baths and bed.
Small Benn has warts. Miss Myra's head
Is full of wool. John L. just said
All the bad words he was never allowed
To use at home. (My, he looks proud!)
And none of us ever mind anymore.
And we drop our things all over the floor.
And we never ever go to bed.
Well, thanks for the shoes."—That's what they said
In the note from India.

                      Their last note
(It was the last good-bye they wrote
As far as we know) was marked "At Sea."
And what it said was: "Since we're free,
We're bound for Australia. That's where we'll be
By the time this letter gets to you.
We are going to catch us a Kangaroo.
Please send us at once a Kangaroo Trap,
Some Pretzels and Pickles, and maybe a Map
With the Kangaroo Places marked in red,
And a Ball of Twine, and a Spool of Thread
(John L. has a rip, and Small Benn's kite
Is out of String). We are all right.
I hope you are sorry we ran away."
It was signed "Miss Myra," and dated "May."

We sent the Twine for Small Benn's kite
Air-parcel-post that very night,
With a Spool of Thread (and a Needle, too,)
For John L.'s rip. But the best I could do
With the Kangaroo Map was a bit of a mess.
I didn't know, so I had to guess

Where the Kangaroo Places were likely to be,
And *all* of Australia looked likely to me,
And even some parts of Alaska and Texas.
Before I was through, there were so many X's
They covered the map so, that no one could tell
What it was a map *of*. I did do quite well
With the Pretzels and Pickles (one tub and one barrel)
Which I wrapped in odd bits of Miss Myra's apparel.
(She had left things behind—in her hurry perhaps.)
So that much was done. But the Kangaroo Traps!—
Oh, those Kangaroo Traps! Have any of *you*
Tried shopping for things that might possibly do
For catching and holding a live Kangaroo?
I finally bought a large cage at the zoo.
At least that would *hold* one, though I couldn't guess
How it might *trap* it—and couldn't care less.

We wrapped it all up. It made quite a pack,
So we sent *that* by ship.

                              In three years it came back
With a letter that read:
                    "Dear Mr. and Mrs.:
By official report (and that is what this is)
Miss Myra and Small Benn and John L.—those three
Have been here and gone. As it seems now to me
They will not be back, as I think you'll agree.
The details are as follows:
                              Small Benn: lost at sea.
Sailed off in a tantrum, split up on a reef.
Some think he attacked it. We share your great grief.

The one called Miss Myra (as far as we know)
Lies buried in ninety-nine inches of snow.
Report states that though it was starting to blow
She went out to buy pickles at forty-below.
We repeat our condolences.

                            That leaves—let's see—
The one called John L. As sworn before me
By rumor and hearsay and witnesses, he
Did say his bad words to a King Kangaroo
That replied with a kick that would certainly do
To put him in orbit, and certainly did.
Once more—our regrets. Postage due, seven quid.
I am, sir and madam, John Jasper MacNeice,
House Painter, Gents' Tailor, and Chief of Police."

We read it straight through, and again, and again
(Once backwards, and once in a mirror) and then,
I looked at Mummy and she looked at me.
And that's when we knew that at last we were free
Of Miss Myra and Small Benn and John L.—those three.
But we fought back our tears and our sorrow, we did.
I counted my money and sent seven quid
(That's twenty-one dollars) to J. J. MacNeice,
House Painter, Gents' Tailor, and Chief of Police.
And Mummy replied with a courteous note,
Taking pains (for politeness) to say that he wrote
A most elegant hand, and she thanked him for that.
And when she was finished, I put on my hat.
And she put on hers. And in silence we two
Walked out through the park, down those paths we both knew,
And—still silent—we paused half a day at the zoo.
For it brought back fond memories—to her and to me—
Of Miss Myra and Small Benn and John L.—those three.

AND HERE'S WHAT HAPPENED LAST
or
HOW MUMMY AND I WERE FINALLY
UNMONSTERED FOREVER

It was seven slow years and three months—to the day—
When I looked at our sundial. It read HALF PAST MAY
Or TWO QUARTERS TO JUNE—whichever you choose.
For we *do* have a sundial, and sundials may use
Any language they please. (How else could they speak
To the Arab, the Chinese, the Finn, and the Greek
To tell them the time?)
                                    And the time sundials tell
May be minutes and hours. But it may just as well
Be seconds and sparkles, or seasons and flowers.
No, don't think of time as just minutes and hours.
Time can be heartbeats, or bird songs, or miles,
Or waves on a beach, or ants in their files
(They *do* move like seconds—just watch their feet go:
Tick-tick-tick, like a clock). You'll learn as you grow
That whatever there is in a garden, the sun
Counts up on its dial. By the time it is done
Our sundial—or someone's—will certainly add
All the good things there are. Yes, and all of the bad.
And if anyone's here for the finish, the sun
Will have told him—by sundial—how well we have done.
How well we have done, or how badly. Alas,
That *is* a long thought. Let me hope we all pass.

Seven slow years had passed. Plus three months—to the day
Since Miss Myra, Small Benn, and John L. ran away.
And Mummy and I had had long thoughts to think.
With only two dishes at once in the sink,

55

The washing took no time, and wiping took less.
And with no one around to leave things in a mess
We had *time* for long thoughts. And the very long-longest,
And also the saddest, and also the strongest
Was—just as you've guessed (for what else could it be?)—
Of Miss Myra and Small Benn and John L.—those three.

But when you start thinking a very long thought
You will find, as a rule, that before you have got
Halfway to the end, you have thought yourself through
—To a nap.

I was napping. And Mummy was, too.
When a rattle-bang-knock at the door broke our peace
—And there stood none other than J.J. MacNeice,
House Painter, Gents' Tailor, and Chief of Police.

"I have come, sir and madam," he said with a bow,
"To bring you some letters that reached me just now.
—Yes, that is rather fast. But the how and the why
Of it all is —I happened to be passing by.
I was out for a stroll, and the first thing I knew
I happened to find I was strolling by you
Which happened to bring to my mind certain metters"
(I think he meant "matters") "concerning three letters
I happened to have in my pocket, which I
Now place in your hand before going my why"
(I think he meant "way") "for I have—do you see? —
To hurry if I'm to get back home for tea."

"It *is* a long stroll," Mummy said. I agreed.
"May I say you have come with remarkable speed?"
I added politely. At which Mummy nodded
(For a pleasant remark really should be applauded.
If that's what you think, we're of one mind with you,
Though the rule to remember is: Don't Overdo).

"Do come in, sir," I said. Replied J.J. MacNeice,
Gents' Tailor, House Painter, and Chief of Police:
"I thank you, but, sadly, I'm forced to decline.
I've a fitting at seven, my dinner at nine,
Some painting to do after dinner, and then
Some police forms to fill out. My business has been
Rather brisk this past season. So if you'll allow,
I'll just leave these letters and start back right now."

—Which he did, after making an elegant bow.
Pausing only to say that the suit I had on
Was very well cut. And again—on the lawn—
To turn a professional eye on the house
And nod with approval and call back to us,
"That's a fine coat of paint!" (He *was* very polite.)

And with that he turned quickly and passed out of sight.
(I *do* hope he got to his fitting all right,
And had a good dinner, for after *that* stroll
He must have been ready to eat an ox whole!)

Well, I looked at Mummy and she looked at me
And we looked at the letters (of which there were three)
And a day and a night and an hour or two more
Flew by. And we still hadn't moved from the door
Nor opened the letters. We just didn't dare.
Till I heard Mummy say, "This will get us nowhere.
And it's starting to rain. Let me put on some tea
While you open the letters and read them to me."

And that's what we did. (She poured and I read.)
I opened the first. "It's from Myra," I said.

"Oh, good," Mummy answered. "With one lump or two?"

59

"Our—uh—daughter," I said. "I think one lump will do."
"There, now," Mummy said as she passed me my tray.
"Don't let it get cold. And what does she say?"

So I drank down my tea and I finished my bread
And I read her the letter, and here's what it said:

"Dear Mummy and Daddy: I think I've caught cold.
And, somehow or other, I think I've got old.
I went out for a walk—it seems ages ago—
And the first thing I knew it had started to snow.
And the next thing I knew I was standing—*kerchoo!*—
In a puddle of slush and was soaked through and through.
Please send me some stuff that is good for a sneeze."

(Here I looked at Mummy and said, "She said 'please'!"
But all Mummy said was, "What else does she need?
We'll discuss manners later. Right now—please—just read."
So I looked for my place and I started again
From—uh—"Good for a sneeze:")
                                    " . . . And a dollar and ten
For a movie and pickles. Would you like to come?
If not, send my plane fare and I'll come straight home
Right after the feature the second time through.
It is, I am told, a fine picture—*kerchoo!*—
By the man who sells tickets, a J. J. MacNeice,
Theater Owner, Head Usher, and Chief of Police.
He also sells dresses—send money for two.
Well, that's all for now. I must close. How are you?
Love—Myra."

            The next was from John L. and read:
"Hi Earthlings! That comet you saw overhead
Was yours truly in orbit! I made it! Please send
Some money for food and some money to spend

60

And some money to have. Mr. J. J. MacNeice,
Travel Agent, Gents' Tailor, and Chief of Police
Is getting the tickets on Flight 93
And has made me a suit. I'll arrive C.O.D.
Pick me up at the airport—and bring a surprise.
Well, regards from the Space Kid to both of you guys.
Signed—Jon'l."

I looked up at Mummy and said,
"Well, nothing has changed!" She nodded her head.
But all she would say was, "Read on." So I read.
The last letter, of course, was from Benn:

"Derest Ded:
I hev bin out two see an I gut my fete wett
But I will cum hom now as soone as I get
The mony you send me. Send it rite awai.
I do nut like geting wett evry dai.
It is two much like bathes. That is all. Yor sun Benn.
(An wen I gett hom plees do nut start agen
Abote bathing and minding and maners becuz
I do nut want things to get back like they wuz.
Luv to Momey. Make chek out to J. J. MacNees,
Shipp's Captin, Dri Guds, and Cheef of Polees.
I own him a debt for a tiket, yu see,
An sum close I wuz needing. Wel, goodby now—Me.")

—Well, I looked at Mummy a very long while.
And she looked at me. With no trace of a smile.
I said nothing to her. She said nothing to me.
An hour must have passed. And then two. And then three.
And then—still in silence—we started upstairs
And packed five valises—two of ours, three of theirs.
And we sent off the three care of J. J. MacNeice,
Miscellaneous Dealer and Chief of Police,

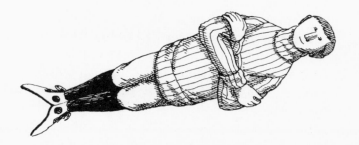

Along with a check that we thought ought to do.
And she got her coat. And I got mine, too.
And we both put them on. And also our hats.
And Mummy her fur piece. And I my best spats.
And I took our valises—one in each hand—
And we started to walk. And we walked. And walked. And
Then walked some more. Till we came to a train.
And got on. And
                    WE NEVER
                              WERE HEARD
                                        OF AGAIN.

                    THE
                    END